Gourmet

POSH TOASTIES

Simple & Delicious Gourmet Recipes For Your Toastie Machine, Sandwich Grill Or Panini Press.

 CookNation

POSH TOASTIES
SIMPLE & DELICIOUS GOURMET RECIPES FOR YOUR TOASTIE MACHINE, SANDWICH GRILL OR PANINI PRESS.

ISBN 978-1-909855-86-1

A CIP catalogue record of this book is available from the British Library

DISCLAIMER

Some recipes may contain nuts or traces of nuts. Those suffering from any allergies associated with nuts should avoid any recipes containing nuts or nut based oils.

This information is provided and sold with the knowledge that the publisher and author do not offer any legal or other professional advice.

In the case of a need for any such expertise consult with the appropriate professional.

This book does not contain all information available on the subject, and other sources of recipes are available.

This book has not been created to be specific to any individual's requirements.

Every effort has been made to make this book as accurate as possible. However, there may be typographical and or content errors. Therefore, this book should serve only as a general guide and not as the ultimate source of subject information.

This book contains information that might be dated and is intended only to educate and entertain.

The author and publisher shall have no liability or responsibility to any person or entity regarding any loss or damage incurred, or alleged to have incurred, directly or indirectly, by the information contained in this book.

CONTENTS

GUILTY PLEASURE SWEET TOASTIES — 73

TOASTIE EXTRAS — 81

OTHER COOKNATION TITLES — 91

INTRODUCTION

If your sandwich maker hasn't seen the light of day for months, dig it out, give it a clean and reward it with pride of place in your kitchen. Toasties are about to get posh.

Posh Toasties' mission is to banish the notion that toastie fillings are nothing more than a slice of tasteless plastic cheese and cheap ham served in questionable cafés up and down the country.

In its place is a vision of culinary toastie treats in every household kitchen. We aim to bring out the very best in your toastie machine, sandwich grill or panini press. Whether you are a student on a budget, a mum looking for a fast, new and exciting snack for the kids, a professional in need of a great weeknight supper or just someone who wants amazing weekend comfort food – there's a posh toastie here for you.

Toasties, made correctly are a fantastic snack, meal or treat any time of the day. Heaven in a sandwich - it's the ultimate comfort food but so much more. With delicious fillings and combinations a regular toastie becomes a gourmet posh toastie in minutes. They're fun to make, simple and don't cost the earth.

Our tasty recipes indulge in delicious meat & seafood fillings, meat free choices, sweet & sticky treats and a selection of simple and easy to make homemade extras like chilli jam, chutney, pesto, hummous and coleslaw. For the sake of simplicity we refer to all the sandwiches in our recipes as toasties, however they can all be made equally successfully using a sandwich grill or panini machine.

If your sandwich maker hasn't seen the light of day for months, dig it out, give it a clean and reward it with pride of place in your kitchen. Toasties are about to get posh!

THE RULES

Rules are made to be broken and our collection of posh toasties push the boundaries in toastie fare but there are a few basic guidelines you should adhere to when making the perfect posh toastie.

Choosing the right bread. Our recipes use different types of bread to mix things up but generally, medium sliced day old bread will achieve the best results – browning nicely and soaking up the ingredients.
Use good quality cheese.
Choose something tangy to compliment.

Be adventurous. Mix and match. Experiment!

'   Season' the plates of your sandwich maker or Panini press. This is important as it will ensure your plates remain non-stick. To do this brush the plates lightly with sunflower oil, close the lid and heat to its highest setting for 5 minutes. It is a good idea to do this periodically to get the best out of your machine.

Always heat up your sandwich maker before adding your sandwich. We recommend the highest setting.

Invest in a heat-proof pastry brush and a heat-proof non-metallic spatula.

Always wear oven gloves when using your appliance. The plates obviously become very hot and fingers can easily be burned if you are not careful.

Either brush your plates or sandwich with oil or butter - our recipes state which.

Avoid using low fat spreads as these can result in your toastie sticking and burning.

Where possible try to leave a small gap around the edges of your sandwich so that ingredients don't spill out onto your machine.

Don't overfill your sandwich. Our recipes create just the right level of fillings but don't be tempted to overdo it as this will inevitably make a mess of your machine.

When making a thicker toastie close the lid slowly applying pressure until it fully closes and/or clicks into place. Do not force the lid shut.

Never cook raw meat or fish in your appliance.

Always read the manufactures guidelines for your appliance.

CLEANING

The great thing about toasties is they are generally simple and easy to make with little cleaning up. Here are a few tips to keeping your machine clean after each use.

* Always unplug the machine before cleaning.
* While the plates are still warm but not hot, wipe with damp kitchen towels to remove any grease.
* Use a non-metallic heat-proof spatula to remove more stubborn residue.
* Use a small sponge with warm soapy water to scrub the plates.
* Wipe dry with kitchen paper towels.
* If the plates can be removed for cleaning make sure they have cooled down first.
* No matter how stubborn the mark, never use any abrasive cleaning products or scourers on the plates of your machine. This will ruin the non-stick coating and render your sandwich maker useless. Persevere with warm water and sponges to remove difficult marks.
* Allow the plates to air dry before closing the lid.

Gourmet

POSH TOASTIES

The Best Meat & Seafood Filled Toasties

⋆⋆⋆★★★★★⋆⋆⋆

Mature Cheddar & Chorizo

Ingredients

SPICY!

2 slices granary bread
50g/2oz sliced mature cheddar cheese
25g/1oz thinly sliced chorizo
Sunflower oil for brushing

First brush your sandwich maker or Panini machine with a little sunflower oil to help prevent sticking and make your toastie nice and crispy. Switch on and bring up to its highest temperature.

Meanwhile arrange the cheese on one piece of the granary bread. Sit the chorizo evenly over the cheese. Place the second slice of bread on top and put into your machine.

Close the lid tightly and leave to cook for 3-4 minutes or until it becomes crispy and golden brown.

Add a little more spice to this toastie with a sprinkle of smoked paprika.

Paprika Spiced Tuna Melt

Ingredients

2 slices granary bread
50g/2oz tinned tuna steak, drained
2 tsp mayonnaise
25g/1oz mature cheddar cheese, grated
1 spring onion, finely chopped

½ tsp paprika
Sunflower oil for brushing

First brush your sandwich maker or Panini machine with a little sunflower oil to help prevent sticking and make your toastie nice and crispy. Switch on and bring up to its highest temperature.

Meanwhile mix together the tuna, mayonnaise, grated cheese, spring onion & paprika in a small bowl. Spread this evenly over one piece of your granary bread. Place the second slice of bread on top and put into your machine.

Close the lid tightly and leave to cook for 3-4 minutes or until it becomes crispy and golden brown.

Smoked paprika is best for this recipe. Alter the quantity to suit your own taste.

Honey Peach & Ham Bloomer

Ingredients

2 tsp butter
2 slices white bloomer bread, thick cut
2 tinned peach halves, sliced
1 tbsp squeezy honey

50g/2oz sliced smoked ham
25g/2oz mozzarella cheese, shredded
Sunflower oil for brushing

Switch on your sandwich maker or Panini machine and bring up to its highest temperature.

Butter the outside of the bloomer slices (the filling will be going on the inside) this will add richness to the toastie and brown it off.

Pat dry the peaches with kitchen roll and combine with the honey in a small bowl.

Arrange the ham & cheese onto one slice of bloomer and add the honey peaches. Place the second slice on top and put into your machine.

Close the lid tightly and leave to cook for 3-4 minutes or until it becomes crispy and golden brown.

You could use fresh peaches for this toastie but tinned are easier to handle.

Parma Ham & Rocket

Ingredients

2 slices white or wholemeal bread
2 tbsp cream cheese
2 slices Parma ham, torn into small pieces

Small handful of fresh rocket
Sunflower oil for brushing

First brush your sandwich maker or Panini machine with a little sunflower oil to help prevent sticking and make your toastie nice and crispy. Switch on and bring up to its highest temperature.

Meanwhile spread the cream cheese over one piece of your bread. Arrange the torn Parma ham and rocket over the cream cheese. Place the second slice of bread on top and put into your machine.

Close the lid tightly and leave to cook for 3-4 minutes or until it becomes crispy and golden brown.

Spinach is also good with this light & tasty toastie.

Creamy Spiced Smoked Salmon Toastie

Ingredients

2 slices white or wholemeal bread
2 tbsp cream cheese
2 tsp horseradish sauce
2 slices smoked salmon, torn into small pieces

Small handful of fresh spinach
Sunflower oil for brushing

First brush your sandwich maker or Panini machine with a little sunflower oil to help prevent sticking and make your toastie nice and crispy. Switch on and bring up to its highest temperature.

Meanwhile mix together the cream cheese & horseradish sauce and spread over one piece of bread. Arrange the torn salmon and spinach over the cream cheese. Place the second slice of bread on top and put into your machine.

Close the lid tightly and leave to cook for 3-4 minutes or until it becomes crispy and golden brown.

Season with plenty of freshly ground black pepper.

Ginger & Lime King Prawn Toastie

Ingredients

2 slices granary bread
50g/2oz mozzarella cheese, shredded
5 cooked king prawns, shelled & chopped
Squeeze of lime

1 tsp freshly grated ginger
Sunflower oil for brushing

First brush your sandwich maker or Panini machine with a little sunflower oil to help prevent sticking and make your toastie nice and crispy. Switch on and bring up to its highest temperature.

Meanwhile mix together the mozzarella, chopped prawns, lime & ginger in a small bowl. Spread this evenly over one piece of your granary bread. Place the second slice of bread on top and put into your machine.

Close the lid tightly and leave to cook for 3-4 minutes or until it becomes crispy and golden brown.

Add some freshly chopped green chilli to this toastie if you like.

Paprika & Lemon Mayonnaise Prawns

Ingredients

2 slices granary bread
Squeeze of lemon juice
1 tbsp mayonnaise
50g/2oz mature cheddar cheese, grated
5 cooked king prawns, shelled

Dash of Worcestershire sauce
Large pinch of paprika
Salt & pepper
Sunflower oil for brushing

First brush your sandwich maker or Panini machine with a little sunflower oil to help prevent sticking and make your toastie nice and crispy. Switch on and bring up to its highest temperature.

Meanwhile mix together the lemon juice and mayonnaise in a small bowl. Add the cheese, prawns, Worcestershire sauce, paprika & seasoning. Spread this evenly over one piece of your granary bread. Place the second slice of bread on top and put into your machine.

Close the lid tightly and leave to cook for 3-4 minutes or until it becomes crispy and golden brown.

If you have fresh herbs to hand add some freshly chopped flat leaf parsley or chives.

Coriander Prawns & Freshly Shredded Carrot

Ingredients

2 slices granary bread
1 tbsp freshly chopped coriander
2 tsp mayonnaise
½ carrot finely shredded/grated
5 cooked king prawns, shelled

Squeeze of lemon juice
Small handful of rocket
Salt & pepper
Sunflower oil for brushing

First brush your sandwich maker or Panini machine with a little sunflower oil to help prevent sticking and make your toastie nice and crispy. Switch on and bring up to its highest temperature.

Meanwhile mix together the coriander, mayonnaise, carrot, prawns, lemon juice & seasoning in a small bowl. Spread this evenly over one piece of your granary bread and arrange the rocket over. Place the second slice of bread on top and put into your machine.

Close the lid tightly and leave to cook for 3-4 minutes or until it becomes crispy and golden brown.

Sesame seeds make a good addition to this toastie.

German Salami & Fig Jam

Ingredients

FRUITY!

2 slices granary bread
1 tbsp fig jam
50g/2oz sliced mature cheddar cheese
25g/1oz thinly sliced German salami
Sunflower oil for brushing

First brush your sandwich maker or Panini machine with a little sunflower oil to help prevent sticking and make your toastie nice and crispy. Switch on and bring up to its highest temperature.

Meanwhile spread the fig jam on one piece of your granary bread. Sit the cheese & salami evenly over. Place the second slice of bread on top and put into your machine.

Close the lid tightly and leave to cook for 3-4 minutes or until it becomes crispy and golden brown.

Fig jam is delicious but any type of strong savoury jam will work well with the salami.

Prawns & Honey Mango

Ingredients

2 slices granary bread
Squeeze of lime juice
½ tsp brown sugar
5 cooked king prawns, shelled & chopped
¼ ripe mango, diced

1 tsp squeezy honey
Small handful of rocket
Salt & pepper
Sunflower oil for brushing

First brush your sandwich maker or Panini machine with a little sunflower oil to help prevent sticking and make your toastie nice and crispy. Switch on and bring up to its highest temperature.

Meanwhile mix together the lime juice, sugar, prawns, mango, honey & seasoning in a small bowl. Spread this evenly over one piece of your granary bread and arrange the rocket over it. Place the second slice of bread on top and put into your machine.

Close the lid tightly and leave to cook for 3-4 minutes or until it becomes crispy and golden brown.

The honey should help bind the filling together.

Bacon & Avocado on Sourdough

Ingredients

1 tsp olive oil
2 slices lean, back bacon
2 slices sourdough bread
50g/2oz mature cheddar cheese, sliced

1 tbsp homemade guacamole (see page 87 for recipe)
Sunflower oil for brushing

First brush your sandwich maker or Panini machine with a little sunflower oil to help prevent sticking and make your toastie nice and crispy. Switch on and bring up to its highest temperature.

Meanwhile heat the olive oil in a non-stick frying pan and fry the bacon until crispy.

Spread the guacamole evenly over one piece of your sourdough bread. Place the cheese and bacon slices on top along with the second slice of sourdough and put into your machine.

Close the lid tightly and leave to cook for 3-4 minutes or until it becomes crispy and golden brown.

Use shop bought guacamole or make your own delicious version using the recipe on page 87.

Blue Cheese & Chicken Bloomer

Ingredients

2 tsp butter
2 slices white bloomer bread, thick cut
1 tbsp full fat cream cheese
50g/2oz blue cheese, crumbled

50g/2oz cooked chicken breast, shredded
Sunflower oil for brushing

Switch on your sandwich maker or Panini machine and bring up to its highest temperature.

Butter the outside of the bloomer slices (the filling will be going on the inside) this will add richness to the toastie and brown it off.

Meanwhile mix together the cream cheese & blue cheese in a small bowl. Spread this evenly over one piece of your bloomer and distribute the chicken evenly. Place the second slice of bread on top and put into your machine.

Close the lid tightly and leave to cook for 3-4 minutes or until it becomes crispy and golden brown.

Try a little blue cheese dressing in this too if you have any to hand.

Burns Night Supper

Ingredients

TRY IT!

2 slices white or wholemeal bread
50g/2oz cooked haggis
50g/2oz mature cheddar cheese, grated
Dash of Tabasco sauce
Sunflower oil for brushing

First brush your sandwich maker or Panini machine with a little sunflower oil to help prevent sticking and make your toastie nice and crispy. Switch on and bring up to its highest temperature.

Distribute the haggis evenly over one slice of bread. Top with the grated cheese and Tabasco sauce. Close with the second slice and put into your machine.

Close the lid tightly and leave to cook for 3-4 minutes or until it becomes crispy and golden brown.

Much maligned for many years, haggis is making a comeback not only in Scotland but all around the world.

Pastrami Reuben On Rye

Ingredients

CLASSIC!

2 slices rye bread
75g/3oz deli pastrami
50g/2oz Swiss cheese, sliced
1-2 tbsp sauerkraut
Sunflower oil for brushing

First brush your sandwich maker or Panini machine with a little sunflower oil to help prevent sticking and make your toastie nice and crispy. Switch on and bring up to its highest temperature.

Meanwhile arrange the pastrami, cheese and sauerkraut evenly over one piece of your rye bread. Top with the second slice of rye and put into your machine.

Close the lid tightly and leave to cook for 3-4 minutes or until it becomes crispy and golden brown.

This is a mountain of a toastie, which is great served with some coleslaw served on the side.

Chicken Breast With Mustard Mayonnaise

2 slices granary bread
50g/2oz cooked chicken breast, shredded
1 tbsp mayonnaise

2 tsp mild French mustard
Small handful of rocket leaves
Sunflower oil for brushing

First brush your sandwich maker or Panini machine with a little sunflower oil to help prevent sticking and make your toastie nice and crispy. Switch on and bring up to its highest temperature.

Meanwhile combine together the mustard and mayonnaise in a small bowl. Add the shredded chicken and mix well. Spread this evenly over one slice of bread and add the rocket leaves.

Top with the second piece of bread, put into your machine, close the lid tightly and leave to cook for 3-4 minutes or until it becomes crispy and golden brown.

If you want a stronger taste opt for English mustard or horseradish sauce instead.

Italian Salami & Pickle Focaccia

Ingredients

1 focaccia roll, sliced in half
2 tsp anchovy paste
50g/2oz Italian salami
50g/2oz mozzarella cheese, sliced

1 gherkin, finely sliced
Sunflower oil for brushing

First brush your sandwich maker or Panini machine with a little sunflower oil to help prevent sticking and make your toastie nice and crispy. Switch on and bring up to its highest temperature.

Meanwhile spread the anchovy paste evenly over one slice of the focaccia. Arrange the salami, mozzarella & sliced gherkin over the paste and top with the second piece of focaccia.

Put into your machine, close the lid tightly and leave to cook for 3-4 minutes or until it becomes crispy and golden brown.

Try using sundried tomato paste if you aren't a fan of anchovies.

Fresh Basil, Swiss Cheese & Ham Toastie

Ingredients

QUICK & EASY!

2 slices white bread
50g/2oz sliced smoked ham
50g/2oz Swiss cheese, sliced
2 tbsp freshly chopped basil
Sunflower oil for brushing

First brush your sandwich maker or Panini machine with a little sunflower oil to help prevent sticking and make your toastie nice and crispy. Switch on and bring up to its highest temperature.

Meanwhile arrange the ham, cheese & chopped basil evenly over one slice of bread.

Top with the second piece of bread, put into your machine, close the lid tightly and leave to cook for 3-4 minutes or until it becomes crispy and golden brown.

You could also try adding some freshly chopped pineapple to this simple toastie.

Fresh Coleslaw & Turkey Breast On Rye

Ingredients

2 slices rye bread
50g/2oz cooked sliced turkey breast
50g/2oz Swiss cheese, sliced

2 tbsp homemade coleslaw (see page 89 for recipe)
Sunflower oil for brushing

First brush your sandwich maker or Panini machine with a little sunflower oil to help prevent sticking and make your toastie nice and crispy. Switch on and bring up to its highest temperature.

Meanwhile arrange the turkey, cheese and coleslaw evenly over one piece of your rye bread. Top with the second slice of rye and put into your machine.

Close the lid tightly and leave to cook for 3-4 minutes or until it becomes crispy and golden brown.

The homemade coleslaw on page 89 is delicious, but of course it's fine to use shop bought if you don't have time to make it yourself.

Parma Ham & Pear on Sourdough

Ingredients

GREAT TASTE!

2 slices sourdough bread
2 slices Parma ham
50g/2oz Gruyere cheese, sliced
1 ripe pear, peeled & thinly sliced
Sunflower oil for brushing

First brush your sandwich maker or Panini machine with a little sunflower oil to help prevent sticking and make your toastie nice and crispy. Switch on and bring up to its highest temperature.

Meanwhile arrange the Parma ham, cheese and pear slices evenly over one piece of your sourdough bread. Top with the second slice of sourdough and put into your machine.

Close the lid tightly and leave to cook for 3-4 minutes or until it becomes crispy and golden brown.

Parma ham is lovely but feel free to use any type of cured ham you prefer.

Lemon Anchovies & Mozzarella Ciabatta

Ingredients

1 ciabatta roll, sliced in half
2 tsp butter, warmed to room temperature
5 anchovy fillets, drained & finely chopped
1 tbsp lemon juice
2 tbsp freshly chopped flat leaf parsley

50g/2oz Mozzarella cheese, sliced
Small handful of spinach
Sunflower oil for brushing

First brush your sandwich maker or Panini machine with a little sunflower oil to help prevent sticking and make your toastie nice and crispy. Switch on and bring up to its highest temperature.

Meanwhile mix together the butter, anchovies, lemon juice and parsley in a small bowl. Spread this mixture evenly over one slice of the ciabatta. Arrange the mozzarella & spinach and top with the second piece of ciabatta.

Put into your machine, close the lid tightly and leave to cook for 3-4 minutes or until it becomes crispy and golden brown.

If you are using a fresh lemon add some of the zest to the butter too.

Chicken & Watercress with Citrus Mayonnaise

Ingredients

2 slices wholemeal bread
1 tbsp mayonnaise
2 tsp lemon juice
½ garlic clove, crushed

50g/2oz sliced, cooked chicken
25g/1oz grated mature cheddar cheese
Small handful of watercress
Sunflower oil for brushing

First brush your sandwich maker or Panini machine with a little sunflower oil to help prevent sticking and make your toastie nice and crispy. Switch on and bring up to its highest temperature.

Mix the mayonnaise, lemon juice & garlic together in a small bowl. Spread this evenly over one piece of bread and lay the chicken, cheese & watercress over. Place the second slice of bread on top and put into your machine.

Close the lid tightly and leave to cook for 3-4 minutes or until it becomes crispy and golden brown.

Turkey or smoked ham works just as well for this fresh, crisp toastie.

Beef & Brocollini Bloomer

Ingredients

2 slices white bloomer bread, thick cut
1 tbsp olive oil
3 anchovy fillets, drained & chopped
1 garlic clove, crushed
50g/2oz tenderstem broccoli, finely chopped

50g/2oz sliced roast beef
25g/1oz mozzarella cheese, shredded
Salt & pepper
Sunflower oil for brushing

Switch on your sandwich maker or Panini machine and bring up to its highest temperature.

Butter the outside of the bloomer slices (the filling will be going on the inside) this will add richness to the toastie and brown it off.

Meanwhile heat the olive oil in a non-stick frying pan and gently sauté the anchovy fillets, crushed garlic & broccoli for a few minutes until softened.

Season well and arrange evenly over one slice of bread along with the beef & grated mozzarella cheese. Place the second slice on top and put into your machine.

Close the lid tightly and leave to cook for 3-4 minutes or until it becomes crispy and golden brown.

Try adding some sliced red peppers to the sauté pan too.

Canadian Maple Bacon Breakfast

Ingredients

2 slices brioche
1 tsp olive oil
2 slices lean, back bacon
1 tbsp maple syrup

50g/2oz Brie, sliced
Sunflower oil for brushing

First brush your sandwich maker or Panini machine with a little sunflower oil to help prevent sticking and make your toastie nice and crispy. Switch on and bring up to its highest temperature.

Meanwhile heat the olive oil in a non-stick frying pan and cook the bacon for a few minutes until crispy. When it's ready pour the maple syrup into the pan, remove from the heat and move the bacon around the pan until coated in the warm maple syrup.

Spread the Brie evenly over one piece of your brioche and add the maple bacon. Place the second slice of brioche on top and put into your machine.

Close the lid tightly and leave to cook for 3-4 minutes or until it becomes crispy and golden brown.

An absolute essential toastie in Canada, this makes a lovely sweet start to the day.

POSH TOASTIES

Gourmet Meat Free Toasties

* * ★ ★ ★ ★ ★ * *

Jalapeno Grilled Cheese on Sourdough

Ingredients

SPICY!

2 slices sourdough bread
50g/2oz mature cheddar cheese, grated
1 tbsp cream cheese
4 roasted jalapeno peppers, sliced
Sunflower oil for brushing

First brush your sandwich maker or Panini machine with a little sunflower oil to help prevent sticking and make your toastie nice and crispy. Switch on and bring up to its highest temperature.

Meanwhile spread the cream cheese evenly over one piece of your sourdough bread. Sprinkle the cheddar on top along with the jalapeno peppers. Top with the second slice of sourdough and put into your machine.

Close the lid tightly and leave to cook for 3-4 minutes or until it becomes crispy and golden brown.

Keep it simple by using jar-bought roasted jalapenos.

Sweet Cannellini & Mustard

Ingredients

- 2 slices granary bread
- 50g/2oz tinned cannellini beans, drained
- ½ garlic clove, crushed
- 2 tsp squeezy honey
- 1 tsp olive oil

- ½ tsp sea salt
- 1 spring onion, finely chopped
- 1 tbsp Dijon mustard
- Sunflower oil for brushing

First brush your sandwich maker or Panini machine with a little sunflower oil to help prevent sticking and make your toastie nice and crispy. Switch on and bring up to its highest temperature.

Meanwhile combine together the beans, garlic, honey, oil, salt, spring onions & mustard in a small bowl. Spread this evenly over one piece of your granary bread. Place the second slice of bread on top and put into your machine.

Close the lid tightly and leave to cook for 3-4 minutes or until it becomes crispy and golden brown.

Smash the beans a little with the back of a fork if you want to slightly bind the filling.

Camembert & Cranberry

Ingredients

STRONG & FRUITY!

2 slices wholemeal bread
50g/2oz Camembert cheese, sliced
1 tbsp cranberry sauce
Small handful of rocket leaves
Sunflower oil for brushing

First brush your sandwich maker or Panini machine with a little sunflower oil to help prevent sticking and make your toastie nice and crispy. Switch on and bring up to its highest temperature.

Mix the cranberry sauce and Camembert together. Spread this evenly over one piece of bread and sprinkle with rocket. Place the second slice of bread on top and put into your machine.

Close the lid tightly and leave to cook for 3-4 minutes or until it becomes crispy and golden brown.

Camembert is a strong tasting soft cheese, particularly lovely when melted.

Grilled Zucchini & Red Pepper Toastie

Ingredients

2 slices white or brown bread
2 courgettes, thinly sliced
2 red peppers, deseeded & quartered

1 tbsp virgin olive oil
1 tbsp green pesto (see page 84 for recipe)

First preheat the oven grill to medium. Brush the peppers and courgettes with olive oil. Season well and place under the grill and cook for 8-12 minutes or until the vegetables are cooked through and a little chargrilled.

Meanwhile brush your sandwich maker or Panini machine with a little more olive oil to help prevent sticking and make your toastie nice and crispy. Switch on and bring up to its highest temperature.

Spread the pesto over one piece of bread. Arrange the chargrilled peppers and courgettes evenly over the pesto. Place the second slice of bread on top and put into your machine.

Close the lid tightly and leave to cook for 3-4 minutes or until it becomes crispy and golden brown.

Red pesto also works well in this simple veggie toastie.

Grated Apple Ploughman's

Ingredients

FRESH & TASTY!

2 slices granary bread
1 tbsp Branston sandwich pickle
50g/2oz sliced mature cheddar cheese
1 apple, peeled & grated
Sunflower oil for brushing

First brush your sandwich maker or Panini machine with a little sunflower oil to help prevent sticking and make your toastie nice and crispy. Switch on and bring up to its highest temperature.

Meanwhile spread the sandwich pickle on one piece of your granary bread. Arrange the cheese and sit the grated apple on top (you don't need to use all the apple if you don't want to). Place the second slice of bread on top and put into your machine.

Close the lid tightly and leave to cook for 3-4 minutes or until it becomes crispy and golden brown.

Use a sweet eating apple not a sharp cooking apple.

Garlic Oil Chestnut Mushroom Toastie

Ingredients

2 tsp olive oil
1 garlic clove, crushed
2 slices white or wholemeal bread
50g/2oz chestnut mushrooms, sliced

50g/2oz mature cheddar cheese, grated
2 spring onions, finely chopped
Salt & pepper
Sunflower oil for brushing

First brush your sandwich maker or Panini machine with a little sunflower oil to help prevent sticking and make your toastie nice and crispy. Switch on and bring up to its highest temperature.

Meanwhile heat the olive oil in a non-stick frying pan and gently sauté the crushed garlic for a minute or two. Add the sliced mushrooms and sauté for a few minutes until softened. Season well and arrange evenly over one slice of bread along with the grated cheese and finely chopped spring onions. Place the second slice on top and put into your machine.

Close the lid tightly and leave to cook for 3-4 minutes or until it becomes crispy and golden brown.

You could add some chopped red onion or chillies to this when you sauté the mushrooms.

Mediterranean Fontina Ciabatta

Ingredients

1 ciabatta roll, sliced in half
1 tbsp sundried tomato paste
1 ripe tomato, sliced

50g/2oz Fontina cheese, sliced
5 olives, sliced
Sunflower oil for brushing

First brush your sandwich maker or Panini machine with a little sunflower oil to help prevent sticking and make your toastie nice and crispy. Switch on and bring up to its highest temperature.

Meanwhile spread the sundried tomato paste evenly over one half of the ciabatta. Arrange the tomato, cheese & olives over the paste and top with the second piece of ciabatta.

Put into your machine, close the lid tightly and leave to cook for 3-4 minutes or until it becomes crispy and golden brown.

Taleggio cheese also works well for this recipe.

Pesto & Mozzarella Ciabatta

Ingredients

1 ciabatta roll, sliced in half
1 tbsp homemade pesto (see page 84 for recipe)

1 ripe tomato, sliced
50g/2oz mozzarella cheese, sliced
Sunflower oil for brushing

First brush your sandwich maker or Panini machine with a little sunflower oil to help prevent sticking and make your toastie nice and crispy. Switch on and bring up to its highest temperature.

Meanwhile spread the pesto evenly over one half of the ciabatta. Arrange the tomato and mozzarella slices and top with the second piece of ciabatta.

Place into your machine, close the lid tightly and leave to cook for 3-4 minutes or until it becomes crispy and golden brown.

Use shop bought pesto if you don't want to make your own.

Stilton & Cranberry Bloomer

Ingredients

TRY ROQUEFORT →

2 tsp butter
2 slices white bloomer bread, thick cut
1 tbsp cranberry sauce
50g/2oz Stilton, crumbled
Sunflower oil for brushing

Switch on your sandwich maker or Panini machine and bring up to its highest temperature.

Butter the outside of the bloomer slices (the filling will be going on the inside) this will add richness to the toastie and brown it off.

Spread the cranberry sauce over one piece of your bloomer and distribute the crumbled Stilton evenly. Place the second slice of bread on top and put into your machine.

Close the lid tightly and leave to cook for 3-4 minutes or until it becomes crispy and golden brown.

This is also good with some shredded cooked chicken or turkey added to the sandwich.

Pesto & Gruyere Ciabatta

Ingredients

ITALIAN FLAVOUR!

1 ciabatta roll
1 tbsp homemade pesto (see page 84 for recipe)
50g/2oz Gruyere cheese, grated
Sunflower oil for brushing

First brush your sandwich maker or Panini machine with a little sunflower oil to help prevent sticking and make your toastie nice and crispy. Switch on and bring up to its highest temperature.

Meanwhile mix together the pesto & grated cheese and spread this evenly over one half of the ciabatta. Top with the second slice and put into your machine.

Close the lid tightly and leave to cook for 3-4 minutes or until it becomes crispy and golden brown.

Use shop bought pesto if you don't want to make your own.

Cioccolato & Basil Brie

Ingredients

SWEET!

2 slices white bread
50g/2oz Brie, thinly sliced
25g/1oz milk chocolate chips
1 tbsp freshly chopped basil
Sunflower oil for brushing

First brush your sandwich maker or Panini machine with a little sunflower oil to help prevent sticking and make your toastie nice and crispy. Switch on and bring up to its highest temperature.

Meanwhile arrange the Brie slices on one piece of your bread. Sprinkle the chocolate chips and basil evenly over the cheese. Place the second slice of bread on top and put into your machine.

Close the lid tightly and leave to cook for 3-4 minutes or until it becomes crispy and golden brown.

Hailing from Italy this unusual combination is a revelation!

Brioche & Dijon Mustard Cheese

Ingredients

TRY ENGLISH MUSTARD!

2 slices brioche bread
50g/2oz sliced mature cheddar cheese
1 tbsp Dijon mustard
Sunflower oil for brushing

First brush your sandwich maker or Panini machine with a little sunflower oil to help prevent sticking and make your toastie nice and crispy. Switch on and bring up to its highest temperature.

Meanwhile spread the mustard over one piece of bread and arrange the cheese over. Place the second slice of bread on top and put into your machine.

Close the lid tightly and leave to cook for 3-4 minutes or until it becomes crispy and golden brown.

The sweetness of the brioche and gentle kick of the Dijon mustard make a great combination in this toastie.

Caponata

Ingredients

2 slices white or wholemeal bread
2 tsp olive oil
½ red onion, peeled and sliced
½ red pepper, deseeded & chopped
1 tbsp sultanas
1 tsp capers, rinsed

1 tsp brown sugar
1 ripe tomato, finely chopped
50g/2oz grated mild cheese
Salt & pepper
Sunflower oil for brushing

Heat the olive oil in a non-stick frying pan to make a simple caponata. Gently sauté the sliced onions, peppers, sultanas, capers, sugar & tomatoes for 6-8 minutes or until soft and cooked through.

Meanwhile brush your sandwich maker or Panini machine with a little sunflower oil to help prevent sticking and make your toastie nice and crispy. Switch on and bring up to its highest temperature.

Quickly stir through the cheese and arrange everything evenly over one slice of bread. Place the second slice on top and put into your machine.

Close the lid tightly and leave to cook for 3-4 minutes or until it becomes crispy and golden brown.

You could make double the quantity and use it to mix with a little boiled rice or couscous for an alternative simple, tasty supper.

Cracked Black Pepper & Caramelized Onions

Ingredients

1 tbsp olive oil
2 slices white or wholemeal bread
1 small onion, peeled and sliced
1 tsp brown sugar

½ tsp dried thyme
50g/2oz sliced mature cheddar cheese
Freshly ground black pepper
Sunflower oil for brushing

First brush your sandwich maker or Panini machine with a little sunflower oil to help prevent sticking and make your toastie nice and crispy. Switch on and bring up to its highest temperature.

Meanwhile heat the olive oil in a non-stick frying pan and gently sauté the sliced onions and brown sugar for a few minutes until softened. Add the thyme and some ground black pepper (enough to suit your own taste) and cook for a minute or two longer.

Layer the cheese on one slice of bread, tip the onions over, place the second piece of bread on top and put into your machine.

Close the lid tightly and leave to cook for 3-4 minutes or until it becomes crispy and golden brown.

A little brown sugar adds a mild sweetness to this simple toastie.

Mexican Chipotle Mushroom & Monterey Jack Cheese

Ingredients

2 tsp olive oil

2 slices white or wholemeal bread

1 large portabella mushroom, sliced

50g/2oz sliced Monterey Jack cheese

1-2 tsp chipotle paste

Salt & pepper

Sunflower oil for brushing

First brush your sandwich maker or Panini machine with a little sunflower oil to help prevent sticking and make your toastie nice and crispy. Switch on and bring up to its highest temperature.

Meanwhile heat the olive oil in a non-stick frying pan and gently sauté the sliced mushrooms for a few minutes until softened.

Spread the chipotle paste over one slice of bread, layer the cheese on top and tip the sautéed sliced mushrooms over.

Season well, place the second slice on top and put into your machine.

Close the lid tightly and leave to cook for 3-4 minutes or until it becomes crispy and golden brown.

Chipotle is the classic Mexican paste but any type of chilli paste/sauce should work well.

Roasted Peppers & Dutch Gouda

Ingredients

2 slices white bread
50g/2oz sliced Gouda cheese
2 roasted peppers, sliced (see page 88 for recipe)

Small handful of rocket or baby spinach
Sunflower oil for brushing

First brush your sandwich maker or Panini machine with a little sunflower oil to help prevent sticking and make your toastie nice and crispy. Switch on and bring up to its highest temperature.

Meanwhile arrange the cheese on one piece of your bread. Sit the peppers and rocket evenly over the cheese. Place the second slice of bread on top and put into your machine.

Close the lid tightly and leave to cook for 3-4 minutes or until it becomes crispy and golden brown.

Use shop-bought jars of peppers if you don't have the time, or inclination, to make your own.

Emmental Cheese With Oak Smoked Ham

Ingredients

2 slices granary bread
1 garlic clove, crushed
50g/2oz sliced Emmental cheese

1 thick slice oak smoked ham
4-5 cornichons, finely chopped
Sunflower oil for brushing

First brush your sandwich maker or Panini machine with a little sunflower oil to help prevent sticking and make your toastie nice and crispy. Switch on and bring up to its highest temperature.

Meanwhile spread the crushed garlic over one piece of bread. Arrange the cheese, ham and chopped cornichons evenly over. Place the second slice of bread on top and put into your machine.

Close the lid tightly and leave to cook for 3-4 minutes or until it becomes crispy and golden brown.

Use thinly sliced and chopped gherkins if you don't have cornichons.

Nutmeg Pears & Cottage Cheese

Ingredients

2 slices white bread
½ ripe pear, peeled, cored & chopped
Large pinch of ground nutmeg

1-2 tbsp cottage cheese
Sunflower oil for brushing

First brush your sandwich maker or Panini machine with a little sunflower oil to help prevent sticking and make your toastie nice and crispy. Switch on and bring up to its highest temperature.

Mix together the pears and nutmeg. Arrange the cottage cheese on one piece of your granary bread. Sit the nutmeg pears evenly over the cheese. Place the second slice of bread on top and put into your machine.

Close the lid tightly and leave to cook for 3-4 minutes or until it becomes crispy and golden brown.

For extra sweetness try adding a pinch of brown sugar to the pears and nutmeg.

Fresh Basil & Vine Ripened Tomato Toastie

Ingredients

2 slices white or wholemeal bread
1 tbsp freshly chopped basil
2 tsp olive oil
2 vine-ripened plum tomatoes, finely chopped

Salt & pepper
Sunflower oil for brushing

First brush your sandwich maker or Panini machine with a little sunflower oil to help prevent sticking and make your toastie nice and crispy. Switch on and bring up to its highest temperature.

Meanwhile mix together the basil, oil, tomatoes & seasoning in a small bowl. Spread this evenly over one piece of your granary bread. Place the second slice of bread on top and put into your machine.

Close the lid tightly and leave to cook for 3-4 minutes or until it becomes crispy and golden brown.

Trying adding some shredded buffalo mozzarella to this fresh & light toastie.

Fresh Cherry & Nut Butter Toastie

Ingredients

2 slices granary or brown bread
2 tbsp smooth peanut butter
1 banana, peeled & sliced

Small handful of ripe cherries, de-stoned & sliced
Sunflower oil for brushing

First brush your sandwich maker or Panini machine with a little sunflower oil to help prevent sticking and make your toastie nice and crispy. Switch on and bring up to its highest temperature.

Meanwhile spread the peanut butter over one slice of bread. Arrange the sliced banana and cherries over the top. Finish the sandwich with the second slice of bread and put into your machine.

Close the lid tightly and leave to cook for 3-4 minutes or until it becomes crispy and golden brown.

Fresh cherries are delicious and best eaten in season.

Portabella Mushroom & Fresh Cherry Tomatoes

2 tsp olive oil
2 slices white or wholemeal bread
1 tsp dried oregano or rosemary
1 large portabella mushroom, sliced

4 ripe cherry tomatoes, finely chopped
Salt & pepper
Sunflower oil for brushing

First brush your sandwich maker or Panini machine with a little sunflower oil to help prevent sticking and make your toastie nice and crispy. Switch on and bring up to its highest temperature.

Meanwhile heat the olive oil in a non-stick frying pan and gently sauté the sliced mushrooms, tomatoes & dried herbs for a few minutes until softened. Season well and arrange evenly over one slice of bread. Place the second slice on top and put into your machine.

Close the lid tightly and leave to cook for 3-4 minutes or until it becomes crispy and golden brown.

Trying adding a little chopped onion when you sauté the mushrooms.

Buffalo Mozzarella, Spinach & Pesto

Ingredients

2 slices wholemeal bread
1 tbsp green pesto sauce (see page 84 for recipe)

50g/2oz buffalo mozzarella, sliced
Small handful of spinach
Sunflower oil for brushing

First brush your sandwich maker or Panini machine with a little sunflower oil to help prevent sticking and make your toastie nice and crispy. Switch on and bring up to its highest temperature.

Meanwhile spread the pesto on one piece of bread. Sit the mozzarella slices and spinach evenly over the cheese. Place the second slice of bread on top and put into your machine.

Close the lid tightly and leave to cook for 3-4 minutes or until it becomes crispy and golden brown.

Watercress and/or rocket are good in this sandwich instead of spinach.

Fresh Houmous & Shredded Chantenay Carrots

Ingredients

VEGGIE CLASSIC! →

2 slices wholemeal bread
1 tbsp houmous (see page 86 for recipe)
2 small Chantenay carrots, finely shredded/grated
Sunflower oil for brushing

First brush your sandwich maker or Panini machine with a little sunflower oil to help prevent sticking and make your toastie nice and crispy. Switch on and bring up to its highest temperature.

Meanwhile spread the houmous over one piece of bread. Sit the shredded carrots evenly over the houmous (don't use all the carrot if it's too much). Place the second slice of bread on top and put into your machine.

Close the lid tightly and leave to cook for 3-4 minutes or until it becomes crispy and golden brown.

Use shop bought houmous if you don't have time to make the homemade recipe on page 86.

Spinach, Feta & Black Olive

2 slices white bread
50g/2oz crumbled feta cheese
½ garlic clove, crushed
Small handful of spinach, roughly chopped

5 black olives, pitted & finely chopped
1 tsp olive oil
Salt & pepper
Sunflower oil for brushing

First brush your sandwich maker or Panini machine with a little sunflower oil to help prevent sticking and make your toastie nice and crispy. Switch on and bring up to its highest temperature.

Meanwhile mix together the crumbled feta cheese, garlic, spinach, olives, olive oil & seasoning in a small bowl. Spread this evenly over one piece of your bread. Place the second slice of bread on top and put into your machine.

Close the lid tightly and leave to cook for 3-4 minutes or until it becomes crispy and golden brown.

Try adding some chopped spring onion if you like.

Avocado, Tomato & Feta

Ingredients

2 slices granary or wholemeal bread
50g/2oz crumbled feta cheese
1 large vine-ripened tomato, sliced
½ ripe avocado, peeled, de-stoned &
sliced

Salt & pepper
Sunflower oil for brushing

First brush your sandwich maker or Panini machine with a little sunflower oil to help prevent sticking and make your toastie nice and crispy. Switch on and bring up to its highest temperature.

Meanwhile spread the crumbled feta cheese over one piece of bread. Sit the tomato & avocado slices over the cheese and season well. Place the second slice of bread on top and put into your machine.

Close the lid tightly and leave to cook for 3-4 minutes or until it becomes crispy and golden brown.

Serve with a large handful of crisp green salad.

The Classic Tricolore

Ingredients

2 slices granary or wholemeal bread
50g/2oz sliced mozzarella cheese
1 large vine ripened tomato, sliced
½ ripe avocado, peeled, de-stoned & sliced

1 tbsp freshly chopped basil
Salt & pepper
Sunflower oil for brushing

First brush your sandwich maker or Panini machine with a little sunflower oil to help prevent sticking and make your toastie nice and crispy. Switch on and bring up to its highest temperature.

Meanwhile lay the mozzarella cheese over one piece of bread. Sit the tomato & avocado slices over the cheese and season well before adding the chopped basil. Place the second slice of bread on top and put into your machine.

Close the lid tightly and leave to cook for 3-4 minutes or until it becomes crispy and golden brown.

Italian in origin, this classic combination mimics the colours of the nation's flag.

Goat's Cheese, Watercress & Sundried Tomatoes

Ingredients

2 slices granary or wholemeal bread
50g/2oz goat's cheese
3 sundried tomatoes, finely chopped

Small handful of watercress
Salt & pepper
Sunflower oil for brushing

First brush your sandwich maker or Panini machine with a little sunflower oil to help prevent sticking and make your toastie nice and crispy. Switch on and bring up to its highest temperature.

Meanwhile spread the goat's cheese over one piece of bread. Sit the chopped sundried tomatoes & watercress evenly over the cheese and season well. Place the second slice of bread on top and put into your machine.

Close the lid tightly and leave to cook for 3-4 minutes or until it becomes crispy and golden brown.

Use sundried tomatoes in oil as these are softer than the dehydrated version, which need soaking in water.

Balsamic Goat's Cheese & Avocado

Ingredients

2 slices seeded brown bread
50g/2oz goat's cheese
½ ripe avocado, peeled, de-stoned & sliced

Small handful of spinach leaves
1 tbsp balsamic vinegar
Salt & pepper
Sunflower oil for brushing

First brush your sandwich maker or Panini machine with a little sunflower oil to help prevent sticking and make your toastie nice and crispy. Switch on and bring up to its highest temperature.

Meanwhile spread the goat's cheese over one piece of bread and drizzle over the balsamic vinegar. Sit the avocado slices and spinach over the top. Place the second slice of bread on top and put into your machine.

Close the lid tightly and leave to cook for 3-4 minutes or until it becomes crispy and golden brown.

Feta cheese also works well for this recipe.

Guacamole & Tabasco Toastie

Ingredients

2 slices wholemeal or white bread
2 tbsp homemade guacamole (see page 87 for recipe)
1 tsp Tabasco sauce

1 vine-ripened tomato, finely chopped
Squeeze of fresh lemon juice
Sunflower oil for brushing

First brush your sandwich maker or Panini machine with a little sunflower oil to help prevent sticking and make your toastie nice and crispy. Switch on and bring up to its highest temperature.

Meanwhile mix together the guacamole, Tabasco, lemon juice & chopped tomato in a small bowl. Spread this evenly over one piece of bread. Place the second slice of bread on top and put into your machine.

Close the lid tightly and leave to cook for 3-4 minutes or until it becomes crispy and golden brown.

Use shop bought guacamole or make your own delicious version using the recipe on page 87.

Turmeric Potatoes & Red Onion

Ingredients

2 slices white or wholemeal bread
2 tsp olive oil
½ red onion, peeled and sliced
1 tsp turmeric

½ tsp cayenne pepper
50g/2oz boiled potatoes, cubed
Salt & pepper
Sunflower oil for brushing

First brush your sandwich maker or Panini machine with a little sunflower oil to help prevent sticking and make your toastie nice and crispy. Switch on and bring up to its highest temperature.

Meanwhile heat the olive oil in a non-stick frying pan and gently sauté the sliced onions for a few minutes until softened. Add the potatoes, turmeric & cayenne pepper, stir well and increase the heat. Cook for a further two minutes before arranging evenly over one slice of bread. Place the second slice on top and put into your machine.

Close the lid tightly and leave to cook for 3-4 minutes or until it becomes crispy and golden brown.

Use less cayenne pepper if you prefer your toastie not to have a kick.

Passata & Mozzarella

Ingredients

2 slices wholemeal or white bread
1 tbsp tomato passata
1 tbsp freshly chopped basil or oregano

50g/2oz mozzarella cheese, shredded
Pinch of salt & brown sugar
Sunflower oil for brushing

First brush your sandwich maker or Panini machine with a little sunflower oil to help prevent sticking and make your toastie nice and crispy. Switch on and bring up to its highest temperature.

Meanwhile mix together the passata, basil, mozzarella, salt & sugar. Spread this evenly over one piece of your granary bread. Place the second slice of bread on top and put into your machine.

Close the lid tightly and leave to cook for 3-4 minutes or until it becomes crispy and golden brown.

The salt and sugar will balance the acidity of the tomatoes in the passata.

Granola, Nut Butter & Honey

Ingredients

BREAKFAST TREAT!

2 slices white bread
50g/2oz granola
2 tbsp smooth peanut butter
1 tbsp squeezy honey
Sunflower oil for brushing

First brush your sandwich maker or Panini machine with a little sunflower oil to help prevent sticking and make your toastie nice and crispy. Switch on and bring up to its highest temperature.

Meanwhile mix together the granola, peanut butter & honey in a small bowl (add a little more peanut butter if needed). Spread this evenly over one piece of your bread. Place the second slice of bread on top and put into your machine.

Close the lid tightly and leave to cook for 4-5 minutes or until it becomes crispy and golden brown.

Use crunchy peanut butter if you prefer the texture.

Homemade Beetroot Chutney & Nut Butter Toastie

Ingredients

TRY CRUNCHY PEANUT!

2 slices granary or brown bread
2 tbsp smooth peanut butter
1 tbsp beetroot chutney (see page 85 for recipe)
Sunflower oil for brushing

First brush your sandwich maker or Panini machine with a little sunflower oil to help prevent sticking and make your toastie nice and crispy. Switch on and bring up to its highest temperature.

Meanwhile spread the peanut butter and beetroot chutney over one slice of bread. Place the second piece of bread on top and put into your machine.

Close the lid tightly and leave to cook for 3-4 minutes or until it becomes crispy and golden brown.

If you don't have time to make your own recipe on page 85 just use shop bought chutney.

Double Gloucester & Cracked Black Pepper

Ingredients

USE EXTRA PEPPER!

2 tsp butter
2 slices wholemeal or granary bread
50g/2oz sliced double Gloucestershire cheese
Freshly ground black pepper

Switch on your sandwich maker or Panini machine and bring up to its highest temperature.

Butter the outside of the bread (the filling will be going on the inside) this will add richness to the toastie and brown it off.

Meanwhile arrange the cheese on one piece of your bread. Grind some fresh black pepper over the top, place the second slice of bread on top and put into your machine.

Close the lid tightly and leave to cook for 3-4 minutes or until it becomes crispy and golden brown.

Try adding some finely chopped red onion to this recipe or a little rocket.

Creamy Dried Apricot Toastie

Ingredients

TRY DATES!

2 slices granary bread
1 tbsp full fat cream cheese
4 dried apricots, finely chopped
Sunflower oil for brushing

First brush your sandwich maker or Panini machine with a little sunflower oil to help prevent sticking and make your toastie nice and crispy. Switch on and bring up to its highest temperature.

Meanwhile mix together the cream cheese and chopped apricots in a small bowl. Spread this evenly over one piece of your granary bread. Place the second slice of bread on top and put into your machine.

Close the lid tightly and leave to cook for 3-4 minutes or until it becomes crispy and golden brown.

Instead of using sunflower oil try spreading the outside of each piece of bread with a little butter for a richer taste to your toastie.

Brie & Best Chilli Jam

Ingredients

SWEET & SPICY!

2 slices wholemeal bread
50g/2oz Brie cheese
1 tbsp chilli jam (see page 82 for recipe)
Sunflower oil for brushing

First brush your sandwich maker or Panini machine with a little sunflower oil to help prevent sticking and make your toastie nice and crispy. Switch on and bring up to its highest temperature.

Spread the chilli jam over one piece of bread, use more or less depending on your own taste. Arrange the cheese on top (either spread or cut into small chunks which will melt evenly across the bread). Place the second slice of bread on top and put into your machine.

Close the lid tightly and leave to cook for 3-4 minutes or until it becomes crispy and golden brown.

Use shop-bought chilli jam or make your own delicious version using the recipe on page 82.

★ ★ ★ ★ ★ ★ ★ ★ ★

Olive Tapenade & Watercress Toastie

Ingredients

2 slices wholemeal bread
1 tbsp olive tapenade (see page 83 for recipe)

50g/2oz mozzarella cheese, sliced
1 small handful of watercress
Sunflower oil for brushing

First brush your sandwich maker or Panini machine with a little sunflower oil to help prevent sticking and make your toastie nice and crispy. Switch on and bring up to its highest temperature.

Spread the olive tapenade over one piece of bread, use more or less depending on your own taste. Arrange the sliced cheese and watercress over. Place the second slice of bread on top and put into your machine.

Close the lid tightly and leave to cook for 3-4 minutes or until it becomes crispy and golden brown.

Use shop bought tapenade or make your own delicious version using the recipe on page 83.

Sunny Side Goat's Cheese Ciabatta

Ingredients

2 tsp olive oil

1 ciabatta roll, sliced in half

1 free range egg

50g/2oz goat's cheese

1 small handful of spinach

Large pinch of sea salt

Sunflower oil for brushing

First brush your sandwich maker or Panini machine with a little sunflower oil to help prevent sticking and make your toastie nice and crispy. Switch on and bring up to its highest temperature.

Meanwhile heat the olive oil in a non-stick frying pan and break the egg into the pan. Cover and leave to cook 'sunny-side' up for a few minutes until the white sets.

Spread this goat's cheese evenly over one half of the ciabatta and sprinkle with spinach. Top with the egg, salt & second piece of ciabatta.

Put into your machine, close the lid tightly and leave to cook for 3-4 minutes or until it becomes crispy and golden brown.

This also works well with cheddar cheese...try adding some sliced fresh peppers too.

POSH TOASTIES

Guilty Pleasure
Sweet Toasties

∗∗∗★★★★★∗∗∗

Caramelised Cinnamon Banana Toastie

Ingredients

1 tbsp butter
2 slices white or wholemeal bread
1 banana, peeled & sliced

1 tbsp brown sugar
Pinch of ground cinnamon
Sunflower oil for brushing

First brush your sandwich maker or Panini machine with a little sunflower oil to help prevent sticking and make your toastie nice and crispy. Switch on and bring up to its highest temperature.

Meanwhile heat the butter in a non-stick frying pan. Add the banana slices and cook on a medium heat for about 30 seconds. Add the sugar and cinnamon, quickly stir around and cook for a minute or two longer until the sugar is melted.

Arrange the bananas evenly over one slice of bread. Place the second slice on top and put into your machine.

Close the lid tightly and leave to cook for 3-4 minutes or until it becomes crispy and golden brown.

Use a slightly under-ripe banana to prevent it turning mushy in the frying pan.

Fresh Strawberries & Hazelnut Chocolate

Ingredients

2 slices wholemeal bread
1 tbsp hazelnut chocolate spread
4-5 strawberries, sliced
½ banana sliced
Sunflower oil for brushing

First brush your sandwich maker or Panini machine with a little sunflower oil to help prevent sticking and make your toastie nice and crispy. Switch on and bring up to its highest temperature.

Spread the hazelnut chocolate over one piece of bread (use more or less depending on your own taste). Arrange the strawberries and banana slices over the chocolate spread, place the second slice of bread on top and put into your machine.

Close the lid tightly and leave to cook for 3-4 minutes or until it becomes crispy and golden brown.

Nutella is a good hazelnut chocolate spread but others are available.

Creamy Fresh Blueberry Toastie

Ingredients

TRY BLUEBERRIES!

- 2 slices wholemeal or white bread
- 1 tbsp cream cheese
- Handful of blueberries
- 1 tsp icing sugar
- Sunflower oil for brushing

1 First brush your sandwich maker or Panini machine with a little sunflower oil to help prevent sticking and make your toastie nice and crispy. Switch on and bring up to its highest temperature.

2 Spread the cream cheese over one piece of bread. Arrange the blueberries over the top and sprinkle with icing sugar. Place the second slice of bread on top and put into your machine.

3 Close the lid tightly and leave to cook for 3-4 minutes or until it becomes crispy and golden brown.

Fresh blueberries can be a little sharp, the icing sugar will take the edge off this.

★ ★ ★ ★ ★ ★ ★ ★ ★

Passion Fruit & Honey Bloomer

Ingredients

- 2 slices white bloomer bread, thick cut
- 1 ripe passion fruit, flesh only
- ½ banana, sliced
- 2 tsp squeezy honey
- Sunflower oil for brushing

1 First brush your sandwich maker or Panini machine with a little sunflower oil to help prevent sticking and make your toastie nice and crispy. Switch on and bring up to its highest temperature.

2 Mix the passion fruit, banana & honey together in a small bowl. Arrange this mixture evenly over one piece of bloomer. Place the second slice of bread on top and put into your machine.

3 Close the lid tightly and leave to cook for 3-4 minutes or until it becomes crispy and golden brown.

You don't have to use all the passion fruit flesh if it's going to make the filling too thick.

Brie & Basil Chocolate Chip Brioche

Ingredients

KIDS' FAVOURITE!

2 slices chocolate chip brioche
50g/2oz Brie, sliced
2 tbsp freshly chopped basil
Sunflower oil for brushing

First brush your sandwich maker or Panini machine with a little sunflower oil to help prevent sticking and make your toastie nice and crispy. Switch on and bring up to its highest temperature.

Spread the Brie evenly over one piece of your brioche and sprinkle with basil. Place the second slice of brioche on top and put into your machine.

Close the lid tightly and leave to cook for 3-4 minutes or until it becomes crispy and golden brown.

Sweet & savoury this toastie also works well with Camembert.

Banana, Honey Fudge Bloomer

Ingredients

2 slices white bloomer bread, thick cut
1 banana, mashed with a fork
25g/1oz soft fudge, finely chopped

1 tsp squeezy honey
Sunflower oil for brushing

First brush your sandwich maker or Panini machine with a little sunflower oil to help prevent sticking and make your toastie nice and crispy. Switch on and bring up to its highest temperature.

Mix the banana, fudge & honey together in a small bowl. Spread this mixture evenly over one piece of your bloomer. Place the second slice of bread on top and put into your machine.

Close the lid tightly and leave to cook for 3-4 minutes or until it becomes crispy and golden brown.

This is a wildly decadent toastie, which is worth treating yourself to now and again.

Ricotta & Fresh Raspberry Bagel

Ingredients

TRY STRAWBERRIES!

1 bagel, sliced in half
50g/2oz fresh raspberries
50g/2oz ricotta cheese
1 tsp icing sugar
Sunflower oil for brushing

First brush your sandwich maker or Panini machine with a little sunflower oil to help prevent sticking and make your toastie nice and crispy. Switch on and bring up to its highest temperature.

Mix the raspberries, ricotta cheese & icing sugar together in a small bowl. Spread this mixture evenly over the bottom half of the bagel. Top with the other bagel half and put into your machine.

Close the lid tightly and leave to cook for 3-4 minutes or until it becomes golden brown.

This can be a little messy but very satisfying!

POSH TOASTIES

Toastie Extras

★★★★★★★★★★

Chilli Jam

Makes 4 Jam Jars

Ingredients

4 red peppers
8 red chillies
6 garlic cloves

750g/1lb 11oz sugar
500ml/2 cups red wine vinegar
4 sterilised jam jars

Deseed the peppers, cut the stalks off the chillies (don't bother deseeding them) and peel the garlic cloves.

Place these into a food processor and pulse until finely chopped.

Add this, along with the sugar and red wine vinegar into a non-stick saucepan.

Bring to the boil and leave to gently simmer for about 50-60mins without stirring. After this time the liquid should be a little thicker and more jam like.

Cook for a further 10-15 minutes stirring occasionally.

Leave to settle for 10 minutes. Divide into sterilised jars, close the lids and leave to cool completely. Should store for at least 8 weeks, refrigerate once opened.

Adjust the amount of chillies to suit your own taste.

Olive Tapenade

Makes Enough For 4-6 Toasties

Ingredients

200g/7oz pitted kalamata olives
4 tbsp extra virgin olive oil
Large bunch of flat leaf parsley

3 tbsp capers
2 garlic cloves
Salt & pepper

Place the olives, oil, parsley, capers & garlic in a food processor and blitz until finely chopped.

Season with salt & pepper and store in the fridge for up to 3 days.

Try adding a twist of lemon juice for a fresher flavour or some anchovy fillets for a deeper flavour.

Homemade Pesto

Makes Enough For 4-6 toasties

Ingredients

Large bunch of basil
100g/3½oz pine nuts
100g/3 ½oz grated Parmesan cheese

380ml/1½ cups olive oil
2 garlic cloves
Salt & pepper

Place the basil, pine nuts, cheese, olive oil & garlic in a food processor with plenty of salt and pepper. Pulse until you have a smooth pesto paste.

Adjust the seasoning, add a little more oil if needed and store in the fridge for up to 5 days.

Feel free to alter the balance of garlic, cheese and salt to suit your own taste.

Beetroot Chutney

Makes Enough For 4-6 Toasties

Ingredients

200g/7oz cooked beetroot
½ red onion, peeled
2 tbsp balsamic vinegar

2 tbsp olive oil
1 tbsp orange juice
Salt & pepper

Place the beetroot, onion, vinegar & oil in a food processor and blitz until finely chopped.

Season with salt & pepper and store in the fridge for up to 3 days.

Use vacuum packed, fresh cooked beetroot for this simple no-cook chutney.

Hummous

Makes Enough For 4-6 toasties

Ingredients

200g/7oz tinned chickpeas, drained
2 tbsp Greek yoghurt
2 garlic cloves
6 tbsp olive oil

1 tbsp lemon juice
2 tbsp tahini paste
1 tsp ground cumin
½ tsp sea salt

Place the chickpeas, yoghurt, garlic, oil, lemon juice, tahini paste & cumin in a food processor and blitz until you have a smooth paste.

Adjust the garlic, lemon and tahini to suit your own taste. Check the seasoning and store in the fridge for up to 3 days.

The Greek yoghurt gives this hummous a rich creaminess.

Guacamole

Makes Enough For 4-6 Toasties

Ingredients

2 avocadoes, peeled & stoned
1 garlic clove, crushed
3 tbsp lime juice

1 tsp paprika
Large bunch of fresh coriander, finely chopped

Cut the avocado flesh into cubes and combine this with the garlic, lime juice, paprika & chopped coriander.

Use the back of a fork to crush some, but not all, of the avocado cubes (so that you are left with a chunky guacamole).

Season with salt & pepper and store in the fridge for up to 3 days.

You could blitz this in a food processor if you prefer a smoother texture.

Roasted Peppers

Makes Enough For 3 toasties

Ingredients

6 red peppers, deseeded & halved
3 garlic cloves, crushed
2 tbsp olive oil

1 tsp dried rosemary
½ tsp sea salt

Preheat the oven to 180C/350F/ Gas 4

Place the peppers, garlic, oil, rosemary & salt in a bowl and combine well to coat each pepper piece in the herby oil.

Lay the peppers out on a baking tray and cook in the preheated oven for approx. 30 minutes or until the peppers are deliciously roasted and cooked through.

Leave to cool. Cover and store in the fridge for up to 3 days.

Yellow or orange peppers are also fine to use, but avoid the more bitter tasting green peppers.

Simple Homemade Coleslaw

Makes Enough For 4-6 Toasties

Ingredients

½ green pointed cabbage
2 carrots, peeled & topped
2-3 tsp Dijon mustard

3 tbsp mayonnaise
4 spring onions

You can either grate/shred the cabbage and carrots before combining with all the other ingredients in a bowl, or alternatively place everything in a food processor and pulse until chopped to the right consistency.

Season with salt & pepper and store in the fridge for up to 3 days.

Fresh and crunchy, you can serve this coleslaw with any of the savoury toasties in this book.

🍎 **CookNation**

Other COOKNATION TITLES

If you enjoyed 'Posh Toasties' we'd really appreciate your feedback. Reviews help others decide if this is the right book for them so a moment of your time would be appreciated.

Thank you.

CookNation is the leading publisher of innovative and practical recipe books for the modern, health-conscious cook.

CookNation titles bring together delicious, easy and practical recipes with their unique approach - making cooking for diets and healthy eating fast, simple and fun.

With a range of #1 best-selling titles - from the innovative 'Skinny' calorie-counted series, to the 5:2 Diet Recipes Collection - CookNation recipe books prove that 'Diet' can still mean 'Delicious'!

Browse our catalogue by searching under 'CookNation' on **Amazon** or visit
www.cooknationbooks.com and **www.bellmackenzie.com**

THE SKINNY SLOW COOKER RECIPE BOOK

Delicious Recipes Under 300, 400 And 500 Calories.

Paperback / eBook

THE SKINNY INDIAN TAKEAWAY RECIPE BOOK

Authentic British Indian Restaurant Dishes Under 300, 400 And 500 Calories. The Secret To Low Calorie Indian Takeaway Food At Home.

Paperback / eBook

THE HEALTHY KIDS SMOOTHIE BOOK

40 Delicious Goodness In A Glass Recipes for Happy Kids.

eBook

THE SKINNY 5:2 FAST DIET FAMILY FAVOURITES RECIPE BOOK

Eat With All The Family On Your Diet Fasting Days.

Paperback / eBook

THE SKINNY SLOW COOKER VEGETARIAN RECIPE BOOK

40 Delicious Recipes Under 200, 300 And 400 Calories.

Paperback / eBook

THE PALEO DIET FOR BEGINNERS SLOW COOKER RECIPE BOOK

Gluten Free, Everyday Essential Slow Cooker Paleo Recipes For Beginners.

eBook

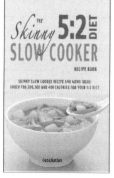

THE SKINNY 5:2 SLOW COOKER RECIPE BOOK

Skinny Slow Cooker Recipe And Menu Ideas Under 100, 200, 300 & 400 Calories For Your 5:2 Diet.

Paperback / eBook

THE SKINNY 5:2 BIKINI DIET RECIPE BOOK

Recipes & Meal Planners Under 100, 200 & 300 Calories. Get Ready For Summer & Lose Weight...FAST!

Paperback / eBook

THE SKINNY 5:2 FAST DIET MEALS FOR ONE

Single Serving Fast Day Recipes & Snacks Under 100, 200 & 300 Calories.

Paperback / eBook

THE SKINNY HALOGEN OVEN FAMILY FAVOURITES RECIPE BOOK

Healthy, Low Calorie Family Meal-Time Halogen Oven Recipes Under 300, 400 and 500 Calories.

Paperback / eBook

THE SKINNY 5:2 FAST DIET VEGETARIAN MEALS FOR ONE

Single Serving Fast Day Recipes & Snacks Under 100, 200 & 300 Calories.

Paperback / eBook

THE PALEO DIET FOR BEGINNERS MEALS FOR ONE

The Ultimate Paleo Single Serving Cookbook.

Paperback / eBook

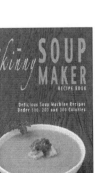

THE SKINNY SOUP MAKER RECIPE BOOK

Delicious Low Calorie, Healthy and Simple Soup Recipes Under 100, 200 and 300 Calories. Perfect For Any Diet and Weight Loss Plan.

Paperback / eBook

THE PALEO DIET FOR BEGINNERS HOLIDAYS

Thanksgiving, Christmas & New Year Paleo Friendly Recipes.

eBook

SKINNY HALOGEN OVEN COOKING FOR ONE

Single Serving, Healthy, Low Calorie Halogen Oven RecipesUnder 200, 300 and 400 Calories.

Paperback / eBook

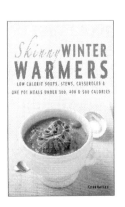

SKINNY WINTER WARMERS RECIPE BOOK

Soups, Stews, Casseroles & One Pot Meals Under 300, 400 & 500 Calories.

Paperback / eBook

THE SKINNY 5:2 DIET RECIPE BOOK COLLECTION

All The 5:2 Fast Diet Recipes You'll Ever Need. All Under 100, 200, 300, 400 And 500 Calories.

eBook

THE SKINNY SLOW COOKER CURRY RECIPE BOOK

Low Calorie Curries From Around The World.

Paperback / eBook

THE SKINNY BREAD MACHINE RECIPE BOOK

70 Simple, Lower Calorie, Healthy Breads...Baked To Perfection In Your Bread Maker.

Paperback / eBook

MORE SKINNY SLOW COOKER RECIPES

75 More Delicious Recipes Under 300, 400 & 500 Calories.

Paperback / eBook

THE SKINNY 5:2 DIET CHICKEN DISHES RECIPE BOOK

Delicious Low Calorie Chicken Dishes Under 300, 400 & 500 Calories.

Paperback / eBook

THE SKINNY 5:2 CURRY RECIPE BOOK

Spice Up Your Fast Days With Simple Low Calorie Curries, Snacks, Soups, Salads & Sides Under 200, 300 & 400 Calories.

Paperback / eBook

THE SKINNY JUICE DIET RECIPE BOOK

5lbs, 5 Days. The Ultimate Kick- Start Diet and Detox Plan to Lose Weight & Feel Great!

Paperback / eBook

THE SKINNY SLOW COOKER SOUP RECIPE BOOK

Simple, Healthy & Delicious Low Calorie Soup Recipes For Your Slow Cooker. All Under 100, 200 & 300 Calories.

Paperback / eBook

THE SKINNY SLOW COOKER SUMMER RECIPE BOOK

Fresh & Seasonal Summer Recipes For Your Slow Cooker. All Under 300, 400 And 500 Calories.

Paperback / eBook

THE SKINNY HOT AIR FRYER COOKBOOK

Delicious & Simple Meals For Your Hot Air Fryer: Discover The Healthier Way To Fry.

Paperback / eBook

THE SKINNY ACTIFRY COOKBOOK

Guilt-free and Delicious ActiFry Recipe Ideas: Discover The Healthier Way to Fry!

Paperback / eBook

THE SKINNY ICE CREAM MAKER

Delicious Lower Fat, Lower Calorie Ice Cream, Frozen Yogurt & Sorbet Recipes For Your Ice Cream Maker.

Paperback / eBook

THE SKINNY 15 MINUTE MEALS RECIPE BOOK

Delicious, Nutritious & Super-Fast Meals in 15 Minutes Or Less. All Under 300, 400 & 500 Calories.

Paperback / eBook

THE SKINNY SLOW COOKER COLLECTION

5 Fantastic Books of Delicious, Diet-friendly Skinny Slow Cooker Recipes: ALL Under 200, 300, 400 & 500 Calories!
eBook

THE SKINNY MEDITERRANEAN RECIPE BOOK

Simple, Healthy & Delicious Low Calorie Mediterranean Diet Dishes. All Under 200, 300 & 400 Calories.

Paperback / eBook

THE SKINNY LOW CALORIE RECIPE BOOK

Great Tasting, Simple & Healthy Meals Under 300, 400 & 500 Calories. Perfect For Any Calorie Controlled Diet.

Paperback / eBook

THE SKINNY TAKEAWAY RECIPE BOOK

Healthier Versions Of Your Fast Food Favourites: All Under 300, 400 & 500 Calories.

Paperback / eBook

THE SKINNY NUTRIBULLET RECIPE BOOK

80+ Delicious & Nutritious Healthy Smoothie Recipes. Burn Fat, Lose Weight and Feel Great!

Paperback / eBook

THE SKINNY NUTRIBULLET SOUP RECIPE BOOK

Delicious, Quick & Easy, Single Serving Soups & Pasta Sauces For Your Nutribullet. All Under 100, 200, 300 & 400 Calories!

Paperback / eBook

THE SKINNY PRESSURE COOKER COOKBOOK

USA ONLY

Low Calorie, Healthy & Delicious Meals, Sides & Desserts. All Under 300, 400 & 500 Calories.

Paperback / eBook

THE SKINNY ONE-POT RECIPE BOOK

Simple & Delicious, One-Pot Meals. All Under 300, 400 & 500 Calories

Paperback / eBook

THE SKINNY NUTRIBULLET MEALS IN MINUTES RECIPE BOOK

Quick & Easy, Single Serving Suppers, Snacks, Sauces, Salad Dressings & More Using Your Nutribullet. All Under 300, 400 & 500 Calories

Paperback / eBook

THE SKINNY STEAMER RECIPE BOOK

Healthy, Low Calorie, Low Fat Steam Cooking Recipes Under 300, 400 & 500 Calories.

Paperback / eBook

MANFOOD: 5:2 FAST DIET MEALS FOR MEN

Simple & Delicious, Fuss Free, Fast Day Recipes For Men Under 200, 300, 400 & 500 Calories.

Paperback / eBook

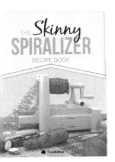

THE SKINNY SPIRALIZER RECIPE BOOK

Delicious Spiralizer Inspired Low Calorie Recipes For One. All Under 200, 300, 400 & 500 Calories

Paperback / eBook

THE SKINNY SLOW COOKER STUDENT RECIPE BOOK

Delicious, Simple, Low Calorie, Low Budget, Slow Cooker Meals For Hungry Students. All Under 300, 400 & 500 Calories

Paperback / eBook

MANFOOD: GYM DIARY:

The Only Pocket Workout Journal You'll Ever Need

Paperback / eBook

THE SKINNY NUTRIBULLET 7 DAY CLEANSE

Calorie Counted Cleanse & Detox Plan: Smoothies, Soups & Meals to Lose Weight & Feel Great Fast. Real Food. Real Results

Paperback / eBook

CONVERSION CHART: DRY INGREDIENTS

Metric	Imperial
7g	¼ oz
15g	½ oz
20g	¾ oz
25g	1 oz
40g	1½oz
50g	2oz
60g	2½oz
75g	3oz
100g	3½oz
125g	4oz
140g	4½oz
150g	5oz
165g	5½oz
175g	6oz
200g	7oz
225g	8oz
250g	9oz
275g	10oz
300g	11oz
350g	12oz
375g	13oz
400g	14oz

Metric	Imperial
425g	15oz
450g	1lb
500g	1lb 2oz
550g	1¼lb
600g	1lb 5oz
650g	1lb 7oz
675g	1½lb
700g	1lb 9oz
750g	1lb 11oz
800g	1¾lb
900g	2lb
1kg	2¼lb
1.1kg	2½lb
1.25kg	2¾lb
1.35kg	3lb
1.5kg	3lb 6oz
1.8kg	4lb
2kg	4½lb
2.25kg	5lb
2.5kg	5½lb
2.75kg	6lb

CONVERSION CHART: LIQUID MEASURES

Metric	Imperial	US
25ml	1fl oz	
60ml	2fl oz	¼ cup
75ml	2½ fl oz	
100ml	3½fl oz	
120ml	4fl oz	½ cup
150ml	5fl oz	
175ml	6fl oz	
200ml	7fl oz	
250ml	8½ fl oz	1 cup
300ml	10½ fl oz	
360ml	12½ fl oz	
400ml	14fl oz	
450ml	15½ fl oz	
600ml	1 pint	
750ml	1¼ pint	3 cups
1 litre	1½ pints	4 cups

Made in the USA
San Bernardino, CA
10 December 2018